Victorious

OVERCOMING THE STORMS OF LIFE

JANICE BENTLEY

Victorious: Overcoming the Storms of Life
Copyright © 2016 by Janice Bentley
Janice Bentley Enterprises, LLC Publishing Publishing
Library of Congress Control Number:
ISBN: 978-0-692-78298-9

All scripture quotations are taken from the New International Version.
Copyright © 2015, Tyndale.

Cover and layout design by Vanessa Mendozzi
Edited by Neecee Matthews-Bradshaw
Printed in the United States of America

Contents

INTRODUCTION

I pray all goes well with you, that you may be in good health, and all goes well with your soul. (3 JN. 1:2)

None of us knows what situations can arise in life. Unpredictably, the winds rise, the sky darkens, and we are in a storm. While one storm can leave devastation in our lives, another brings growth and spiritual development. There are storms we can all encounter:

- Storms we engineer by our foolishness or disobedience. Like Jonah got into when he tried to flee from the presence of God.
- Storms God sends for growth. Jesus commanded His disciples to get into a boat to go to the other side of the sea. He knew a storm was brewing, but was teaching them a lesson for their spiritual development.
- Storms we're brought into through other people, here also is a lesson or opportunity for spiritual growth.

Read my journey and understand you can be called to endure storms as a soldier of Jesus Christ. My journey demonstrates endurance and preparation for movement into a greater destiny. It offers hope and strength to anyone struggling to deal with storms in their life. I believe God is bringing glory to His name. Read and learn to humble yourself under the hand of God and give any anxieties to Him.

That God's way may be known, and His saving power among all nations. (Ps. 67:2)

God is there for you!!

God gives power to the faint, and to those without might He increases in strength. (Isa. 40:29)

When it seems like your world is falling apart, God has a purpose!!

A PRAYER

I thank you, dear Lord, for the saving and healing grace that is found in Jesus Christ, our Lord and Savior. I pray for those who may be struggling with situations in their lives and may feel overwhelmed by them. I pray that they turn to and accept the saving grace and strength that is found in Jesus' power. I know the saving grace and salvation you offer to anyone who draws near to you asking Jesus to come into their life and accepting you as their Lord and Savior. They are saved and given a new life that comes from knowing Jesus; the old is passed away, giving way to the new redemption. I know you will hear them and never turn them away. As anyone comes to you I know that you will bring them salvation, peace, hope, and restoration in the midst of their life struggles. I honor you and adore you. It's in Jesus' mighty name I pray, AMEN!

Chapter 1

The Storms of Life – "Pop Quizzes"

Have you ever experienced, or are you now experiencing, a life-altering storm that has taken you by surprise and really rocked your world? I have, and I know this kind of situation can literally mess with your head. Well, guess what? You've been given a life class pop quiz. And the Master Teacher is challenging you to prepare to advance beyond the material He has already exposed you to and stretch you to a new level of experiences that will propel you into your destiny. His plan is designed, I believe, to get you where you need to be by building you up step by step on your journey.

Will you fail the pop quiz and need a review of all the class material that the Master Teacher has already provided or sought to teach you from The Book of Life, which you were exposed to previously during class?

Although you had the material that was prepared and presented to you during class, maybe you didn't follow the outline given to you, you didn't study the notes that you took, or perhaps you took no notes, maybe not enough notes, or you just didn't internalize and understand the material He presented to you. Either way, if you fail a pop quiz you may need to study the lessons harder, take more or better notes, pay closer attention to what's being presented in class, or maybe even get with a study group. And then, the next consideration becomes;

Are you going to be prepared for the bigger tests that are sure to come?

I have learned that every storm in life is a test, a building block. And there is a lesson to be learned from each one. As you continue to advance to the next level in the storms of your life, you will have to be prepared to build from the material you have already been given and had the opportunity to learn from. We all have to encounter storms or tests, and they can come suddenly. The outcomes of our encounters depend how we prepare to face these storms (our attitude), and our attitude is everything if we are to be triumphant.

It has been said that the bitter experiences we endure are one of the best teachers we have in life.

Adverse surprises or storms of life are tests or challenges that I compare to a sudden tornado containing devastating destructive winds that come out of nowhere. The storm forces anyone in its path to run for a safe shelter in an attempt to escape the disturbance that has suddenly turned a peaceful environment into one of utter chaos. The best thing to do is to run to the safe refuge that is found in Jesus Christ, a very present help in the turbulent storms of life (Psalms 46:1-2). You will endure and pass the worst of the storms of life if you are properly rooted in Christ, who is always available to help you. You must understand that, and you have to trust Him to successfully get you to the place needed in order to pass the smaller pop quizzes and then be prepared to advance to the larger ones. Then you will be like a strong tree in a rough storm because the strongest trees survive; they may bend a little, lose some branches and leaves, but they remain standing. Most of that can be attributed to the deep root system they have developed that serves as an anchor.

Like a tree, you may lose some leaves and branches and bend, but you will return to an upright position and endure because of the durability and flexibility that you have developed in Christ, qualities that enable you to handle the very worst with relatively minor, if any, damage. Like a tree you might be shaken in your storms of life, but the best thing I have found to do is to make sure to always stay anchored in the safe refuge that is found in Jesus Christ, a very present help in the turbulent storms of life (Psalms 46:1-2).

Everything cast against you God is making into artillery in your hand to endure any future storms that may come against you.

You must understand and learn that enduring each storm builds you up and allows you to keep on keeping on in spite of whatever happens in your life. This calls for an act of faith in our Lord. I think about the disciples who encountered the storm while Jesus was right there on the boat with them (Matthew 8:23-27). These hand-picked students—who knew Jesus and had been with him, witnessed his miracles, and heard his messages—were short on faith at that stressful moment. I believe we can all have those moments. And it's during these times we need to stop, pray, and put everything into perspective and believe God is right there with us in our storm. Like the disciples, you have taken your eyes off the One who is right there with you in your storms and is more than able to calm the tempestuous situations in your life, as He did with the disciples (Mark 4:37-40). You've got to keep in mind that Jesus wasn't surprised by that storm, or ours, and I believe in the midst of our storms He is growing us, preparing us to move into our destiny.

Jesus asked the disciples, and I ask you to ponder: Why are you fearful? Do you have Faith?

With just a few words, Jesus can calm any storm in your life, and Jesus has a far better future or outcome for us than we can ask or think. Just as Jesus rescued the disciples from the storm, he is also more than able to rescue us from the storms that arise in our lives, whether they be sickness, loss of a job, loss of finances, marital problems, the pain of death of a loved one, or whatever else they may be.

God is allowing you to experience a time of growth and faith in Him.

Jesus warns us that in this life we will have trials and tribulations, but we must remain courageous (John 16:33). As God told Joshua to be strong and very courageous, "because I am with you", so shall He be with you also. Jesus will never leave us or forsake us (Joshua 1: 5-6). God is right there with us; we are not alone! God is near to the broken-hearted and saves those who feel crushed in their spirit (Psalms 34:18).

God's promises are genuine. Meditate on them and remain strong!

God's word tells us in this life we will have trials and tribulations. (John 16:33)

Chapter 2

Expect a Storm Season within Your Lifetime

I know the storms of life can be a major shocker. I believe it is important to prepare our minds and hearts for the inevitable trials of life,
but even with a theological foundation in place for how to face such
storms we can sometimes be shaken or blown over by the fierceness of
the storms when they arrive. My storms came in the form of negative
health issues relating to my heart. And as a result of these negative
heart issues, things I had going on in my life that I really cherished at
that time began to be stripped from me. Initially, this loss of these things
and these new trials were extremely challenging: Losing a 3 bedroom/
2.5 bath house; the inability to work, as I had for 32 years as a flight
attendant with Delta Airlines, flying around the U.S., Latin America,
and Europe; the inability to serve as a training instructor with Delta;
the loss of the CPR training business I owned and operated and my
work as a RN.

Having a theological foundation means knowing what you believe about God, His sovereignty, and the expectation of having some of life's hardships. By studying the scriptures, we can learn more about God, who He is, and His character. It will change one's perspective on how God is perceived in one's time of storms, either negatively or positively.

Rejoice in hope, be patient in tribulation, but constant in prayer. (Romans 12:12)

Even when it seems like your world is falling apart, God has a purpose!!

At first I was struggling with accepting everything that was going on, and, although hard to deal with, this situation forced me to ask myself several questions and ponder on the answers:

1. **Do you trust God?**
2. **Do you believe that God will bring you out victoriously? (Deuteronomy 20:4)**
3. **And also do you believe that He has a specific plan for your life and is preparing you for that plan? (Romans 1:1)**
4. **Do you believe God's plan is more valuable than the stuff which you previously acquired?**
5. **Do you believe God will at the appropriate time return to you double that of which you once had? (Isaiah 61:7)**
6. **What do you believe about God's sovereignty?**

7. **Do you trust that He will use all things, even your storms for your good and His glory?**

8. **How can I trust in and find hope in his sovereignty?**

Those that trust in God will always have to face hardships in many forms. But don't allow them to cause you to have fear. God has not abandoned you. It's impossible to be separated from the love of Christ. (Romans 8:35-39)

I had to learn how to patiently endure my storms and hold on to the belief that God was using all that was happening in my life for my good and as preparation to move me into what was preordained for my life.

Before God formed me in my mother's womb He knew me and had a definite plan for my life. (Jeremiah 1:5)

God's timing is impeccable and used to accomplish His plans. At the intended time, His plan will come to pass, as will His intended results. It's all for the good and not bad. At the conclusion of it all, I will be better equipped for the service He has for me, as will you in your case. I believe my latter days are going to be much better than my former ones. And there will be a double reward that far outweighs what I once considered significant (Job 42:12).

The book of Job in the Bible is about Job, who is the main character of the book. Job is a righteous, God fearing, obedient, upright, and greatly blessed man. Job experiences calamity and suffering that result

from the evil works of Satan, who is intent on getting Job to curse
God. Satan is given permission by God to inflict physical pain and
negative situations upon Job (i.e., the death of his children, servants,
and donkeys; the theft of all of his livestock; and, ultimately, his physical
affliction with painful sores from the soles of his feet to the crown of
his head). In all that Satan was permitted to do, God would not allow
Satan to destroy Job. Even though God allowed Satan to torment Job,
I believe God considered Job one of His show pieces. Because of Job's
faithfulness, God had specific good plans for the eventual outcome of
his situation.

The Book of Job is a model of trust and obedience to God!

Setbacks, tragedies, and sorrows strike Christians and non-Chris-
tians alike. A greater question is in our tests and trials: Can God trust
you to express your faith to the world? How will you respond to your
troubles? Can God use you? Or will you have a victim mentality and
ask God, "Why is this happening to me?" My suggestion is to check
yourself as I had to do!

**What's happening may be beyond our understanding. But
God is never caught off guard by our personal storms but is
always compassionate!**

Job struggled to understand why all this was happening to him,
and it was evident that he was not meant to understand why all of the

negative situations were occurring or why he would have to face these life altering storms without knowing why. In these times, we will have to carry on without knowing why, but just take it one day at a time. Job's suffering was a test for him. It is an example of faithfulness because as he loses everything important to him, he still remains faithful to God. This story illustrates God's sovereignty and Job's faithfulness during a time of great suffering.

Will you trust God no matter what? Or will you allow Satan to bombard your mind with thoughts that God doesn't care? Resist the devil and he will flee from you! (James 4:7)

If you are struggling to grab hold of that belief, it's time for you to examine your belief system! I had to build up my courage so that I could pass all the pop quizzes and have inner peace. What helped me was remembering everything concerning Job's story and God's majesty.

The ultimate victory over adverse situations has already been won for us. (John 16:33)

You may have a lack of understanding, as I once did, and question why something is happening in your life. I didn't realize it at the time, but the enemy was bombarding my thoughts, planting negative thoughts and, initially, causing me to doubt God's good promises.

Watch out for the deception of the devil, and don't allow yourself to trip! He is the major deceiver!!!

Make the devil out to be the liar he is, and trust in the Lord no matter what. Rest in the peace of God, and the peace of God that surpasses all understanding will guard your heart and mind in Christ Jesus (Philippians 4:6-7). It may take some effort, as it once did for me, but learn to hold on to the promises of God and it will help firmly establish your faith.

Make faith and hope your two best friends!

Even though you don't see the evidence of a favorable outcome, there is a blessing mixed up in your storm. The sun will shine again, and even brighter! Get your shades ready because your future is so bright, and you are going to need them. God gives His angels watch over us to keep those who trust in Him in spite of what happens in their lives (Psalms 91:11-12). We must move over and allow God to do the driving! He's our spiritual GPS, knows the road ahead, and can navigate us through the potholes and the sharp twists and turns in the road. God gives us what we need and he has given us the power within ourselves to be triumphant.

Don't have a "woe is me" mentality, confuse the enemy, raise up and send the praise up!

None of us knows what our future has in store for us, but if we know the One who knows our past and our future no matter what storms appear in our lives, we have a secured future. You can't change what has happened, but you can change how you allow it to affect you! It's a fact: we can allow the life courses (the storms) of life to build us up, or, if we allow the enemy to cause us to fret and fear, they will tear us down. Notice I said *allow*. God will give you the power and courage to overcome adversity.

You must have the mindset that you are a conqueror in Christ Jesus (Romans 8:37)

Develop an active prayer life. Do it always before storms hit, during the calm seasons of life. It will help us not only grow in prayer, but also help us remember to go first to God in all things. As we develop our prayer life, prayer will become more instinctual in our crisis.

We will always be triumphant due to the love God has for us.

Be of good cheer (Acts 23:11). There's a blessing in the midst of your storms.

Lo children are God's gifts, a heritage and fruit of the womb. (Psalms 127:3)

Chapter 3
A Family Legacy

- Legacy can be defined as an inheritance; something that is prearranged and is meant to be given to an individual or individuals, and is passed to the intended at a particular time.
- Legacy can also be defined as something that is transmitted or received from an ancestor or predecessor that is passed on to other family members.
- In the theological sense, legacy refers to receiving an irrevocable gift with an emphasis on the special relationship between the benefactor and the recipient and, of course, orchestrated by God.

I was left an unexpected health legacy, and I do not say this as a complaint, only as a reality. A legacy predestined according to the purpose of Him who works all things after the counsel of His own will. My grandmother, Leola E. Haynes, had cardiovascular disease. She, in turn, passed the genetic predisposition of heart problems to her only child, a daughter, my mother, Willa Mae Bentley. The genetic predisposition along with the heart problems passed down as an inheritance to me.

As a result of their cardiovascular (heart) issues, my grandmother, first, and my mother, second, have gone on to live with the Lord after suffering heart attacks. It was challenging to deal with, but they were strong Christian women and both were instrumental in my acceptance of Jesus Christ as my Lord and Savior. My father, James L. Bentley, Sr., had no known family heart issues, and he is still living today in fair health for his 89 years of age.

Cardiac diseases are disorders of the heart and blood vessels and include coronary heart disease, cerebrovascular disease, rheumatic heart disease, congenital heart disease, heart failure, and other conditions. Combined, heart attack or stroke affect more than 1.5 million Americans each year. And although the rate of death has declined over the years, heart disease remains the number one killer of adults, causing 1 in 6 deaths in the U.S. in 2008[1].

My early life held no conclusive indication of the impending heart problems I would later have in life. However, during their youth, two of my siblings did have heart murmurs that were later resolved with medical treatment. And for them no other heart problems developed. As I stated, my family history does reveal a genetic predisposition to heart problems. And there is not a definitive indication as to what person will specifically manifest major heart problems.

From what I have researched from genetic medical sources, and as I

---

1. Heart Disease: Scope and Impact." The Heart Foundation, 2016. http://www.the-heartfoundation.org/heart-disease-facts/heart-disease-statistics/. Accessed 6 September 2016.

understand the information, there is an indication that researchers are still making discoveries surrounding genetic tendencies in some families with heart disease. There is a 50/50 probability of a particular family member acquiring the genetic variations (mutations) to heart disease[2]. Particular environmental influences (such as lifestyle) and behavioral factors which could have also played a part and indicated high risk factors for me. I began smoking as a teen (which is a major risk factor for cardiovascular disease), I had an unhealthy diet (I liked to eat fried and high calorie fatty foods), I had a lack of regular exercise, and I was overweight. All of these helped present a large opportunity for the likelihood that I, as a family member could acquire or inherit cardiac problems, which I of course did. However, it could have gone either way; none of my siblings or other immediate family members have manifested this problem and possibly will never have heart disease.

I choose to believe that my heart problems were an assignment from God for me to break this generational curse off my bloodline. I also see my heart problems as a trial for me, designed to further strengthen my trust in God. He alone is the one who holds my life's destiny. God knew me before I was born or even conceived. He made me, thought about me, and He knows why He created me. He has a definite plan for my life. God knows exactly what He created for me to accomplish and how that will be carried out.

---

2. How Does Heart Disease Run in Families?" Educational Videos | Ambry Genetics: Cardiology, 2016. www.patients.ambrygen.com/cardiology/resources-for-you/educational-videos. Accessed 6 September 2016.

It's important to understand as I have, that although you may not have an understanding of why what is happening to you is happening, it's purpose, or the particular service God preordained for you; nevertheless, it is what it is, and like it or not, you can't dismiss or run from your destiny. (Jeremiah 1:5)

Image 1: The author's maternal grandmother, Leola E. Haynes

Image 2: The author's mother, Willa Mae Bentley

Image 3: The author's father, James L. Bentley, Sr.

I was sick and you (God) came to me. (Matthew 25:36)

Chapter 4
Health Challenges

My health challenges, the storms, began first with the diagnosis of cardiomyopathy (an enlarged heart), which was an indication of the early stages of heart failure. To me, this seemed to appear very suddenly because I had no previous, apparent, ongoing heart problems. As I later learned, that was because sometimes people who have cardiomyopathy never have any signs or symptoms in the early stages of the disease. (It should also be noted, and understandably so, that this lack of signs is why doctors are so concerned with family history.)

Nothing abnormal that was heart-related had ever been noticed earlier in me, and, as I remember, there were never any specific heart-related tests done during any previous physicals (you know those pesky insurance non-payment guidelines for extra testing without an indication of need). I assume because I showed no symptoms to suggest the need for special testing, no tests were done during previous physicals.

My Cardiomyopathy was first diagnosed in 2004. I had just returned home to Atlanta from a church conference in Savannah, Georgia. While in Savannah I began to have shortness of breath during any type of exercise; there was also intermittent swelling in my feet. I could only sleep if I was propped up in bed. Otherwise I would encounter difficulty breathing properly. I knew I was retaining fluid, but I didn't realize how serious the cause was. Upon arriving home to Atlanta, I immediately went to see my doctor who was a general practitioner. She ordered tests including a chest x-ray. Following the test results, she immediately wanted me to see a cardiologist, a heart specialist.

The cardiologist quickly scheduled me for a series of tests—which included blood tests, another chest x-ray, an EKG, an exercise stress test, a heart catheterization, and an echocardiogram. These tests would determine the nature of the problem with my heart, or it's arteries and ventricles, and to measure the pressure and blood flow in my heart. It was believed that the ventricles of the heart may have lost some of their power to pump blood to the body or relax and fill with blood. All the tests would help determine if there was heart failure, the degree or severity of heart failure, the type of heart failure (either systolic or diastolic failure), and the class of heart failure I had (it places a person in heart class functioning categories). The tests would also determine what treatments would be most effective.

The testing gave a definitive diagnosis of cardiomyopathy with the early stages of heart failure. I was started on a series of medications to help treat the problem. The goals were primarily to treat and decrease the likelihood of disease progression and help me to continue to have an acceptable functional quality of life. The medication prescribed at the time was adequate enough to do that for a while.

At this time, I only saw problems, not Godly possibilities. God wants us to see situations the other way around. We should see possibilities, not problems.

Turn to God's word for comfort when everything goes awry.
(Psalms 55:22)

Chapter 5

Other Storms on the Horizon

God knows who will experience gloomy times. It can be sickness, grief, disappointment, or sorrow. He knows we can become overwhelmed by the storms of life brewing within and around us. But meditating on His words found in the Bible, we can come in from the storms and find peace in Him in spite of the swirling winds.

BAM! Another storm hit in my life in December of 2008. I was living in Atlanta at the time, working as a flight attendant with Delta Air Lines, the largest airline based there, when I had a stroke. It was a Sunday after church, and I had gone home, where I lived alone, and was relaxing. Thank goodness a friend had stopped by. We were having a conversation, catching up on what had been going on in our lives, and after some time (according to my friend) I began slurring my words, and my face became distorted, and I slid off the ottoman where I was sitting. And after many attempts to get up, I could not. I had no idea what was going on, and neither did my friend, who obviously was caught off guard. She called another girlfriend of ours, Linda, who lived two houses away to come over and help ascertain what was happening. When Linda got there and saw me, she obviously knew what was happening and immediately called 911. Everything was hazy for a while, and the next thing I remember is being in the hospital and told I had suffered a stroke.

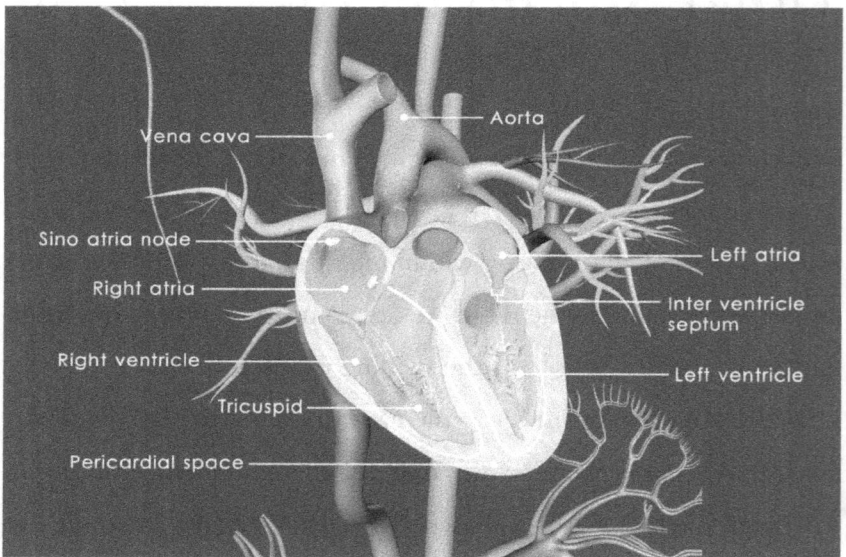

Vena cava — Aorta

Sino atria node — Left atria

Right atria — Inter ventricle septum

Right ventricle — Left ventricle

Tricuspid

Pericardial space

The stroke was caused by atrial fibrillation. *Atrial fibrillation* is a very common type of heart arrhythmia, but because it causes an irregular, and fast, heartbeat, it is also very serious. (Normally, the heart beats in a strong, steady rhythm). In atrial fibrillation there is a problem with the heart's electrical system; it has gone haywire, causing an abnormal heart rhythm of quivering, or fibrillation, of the two upper chambers of the heart (the right and left atria).

The right chamber (the right atrium) houses a group of cells called the sinus node, which is the heart's natural pacemaker, responsible for producing a normal orderly heartbeat and rate that pumps blood out of the heart to be circulated throughout the body.

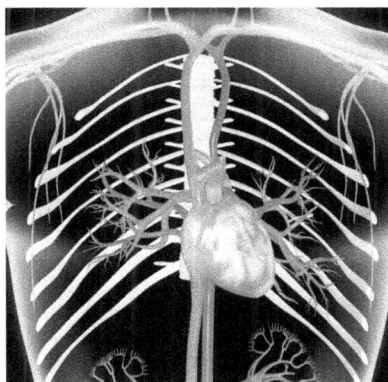

The quivering or fibrillation of the heart upsets the normal rhythm between the atria and the lower parts of the heart, the ventricles. This makes the heart pump blood less effectively as well as weakening the heart; as a result, because the heartbeat isn't strong and steady, blood collects, or pools, in the atria. And pooled blood is more likely to form blood clots. Clots can then travel to the brain, block blood flow there, and cause a stroke, which affects normal functioning and use of certain parts of the body[3]. Which is exactly what happened to me.

I had to believe no matter what, I was safe with God! (Psalms 46:1)

The stroke was yet another storm (a doozy), and hard to deal with. It literally messed me up!!!! But as I realized that I could have died, I understand how blessed I am to still be here.

3. "What is Atrial Fibrillation (AFib or AF)?" The Heart Association: Conditions, July 2016. www.heart.org/HEARTORG/Conditions/Arrhythmia/AboutArrhythmia/What-is-Atrial-Fibrillation-AFib-or-AF_UCM_423748_Article.jsp#.V7UQpigrLIU. Accessed 6 September 2016.

The Lord is our hiding place, and will protect us in trouble and surround us with His favor just like a shield that has the power to protect life! (Psalms 32:7)

Nevertheless, for a time I felt discouragement, and I began to question God. I attempted to rationalize why I was experiencing all of the losses I mentioned earlier. Was it something I did or shouldn't have done that would explain why all this was happening, especially after I had a stroke?

The stroke caused me to first relinquish the spoils of my earthly work. I had to go on a temporary disability leave from Delta, causing me to relinquish those accomplishments, which were, at the time, very significant to me. Now they are all insignificant.

The stroke affected the left side of my body and left me partially incapacitated on that side and in a wheelchair for several months. My speech was affected, and I could not speak very well. For a time, I had to live at a rehabilitation facility while I re-learned the best way to do some of the basic everyday things we automatically take for granted. Toileting became difficult, showering, washing up, dressing, cooking, washing clothes, etc. And since I lived alone during this time, there was a concern for how I was going to continue to live in my house on my own.

My family was, at first, very adamant that I come back to Chicago, where I grew up, to live among family members. They finally accepted the fact that I was determined to stay in Atlanta where I had relocated.

Besides, my good friend Linda, who lived two houses away, assured them that she would be able to help me. It was also a blessing that I had earlier, on a whim, taken out long-term care insurance, which partially paid for a caregiver to come in during the day to assist me. But when there was no one there, I was virtually alone (except, of course, for my guardian angels). Linda was true to her word. She checked on me at night and also spearheaded a campaign that solicited other sister friends to take turns coming over to assist me, with some even staying the night. I thank God for each and every one of them. I was blessed to know them and have their assistance.

As time progressed, can you believe God graced me to be able to drive myself around and many times alone? People were amazed, and so was I. I was able to keep my house for a while until a rusted pipe began leaking and spraying water underneath the house, (unbeknownst to me). And how could I have known? I wasn't one to go under the house, even when I had the ability to do so! Mold developed, and breathing the air in the house became dangerous. And wouldn't you know it, the insurance company had a loophole in my policy and would not pay for any of the damage. I could not afford to pay for correcting everything and, with no substantial income, a loan was impossible. So I had to sell the house as a short sale due to my inability to fix and maintain it. But I thank those who helped me maintain it up to the point of sale. They did so much and out of the goodness of their hearts. Especially Art, a friend's husband, who would faithfully come and cut the grass every week, expecting nothing in return. However, as I prepared to move out of the house, I eventually had to sell or give away some of my possessions. The remaining items in my possession, I put in storage as I worked out where I would ultimately end up living.

God will supply every need of ours.

For a short time, I felt like a homeless person, and that is not a good feeling, moving around from place to place. But God was watching out for me. If you believe the Word of God, the Bible tells us that God is a wonder, and we won't always understand or comprehend God's reasoning behind what happens in our lives.

God's plans are not our plans and neither are our ways His ways. (Isaiah 55:8)

By faith, accept that God's works are always perfect. Learn, as I did, to get a positive vision of your negative situation. In order to do that, you have to trust God's strategy for you overcoming your storms.

And then another storm hit in 2011. Because of the A-fib, I needed to have a battery-operated device, an internal cardioverter defibrillator (ICD), implanted underneath my skin on the upper left side of my chest, above my heart and just below my collarbone

The ICD was a suggested remedy, due to the conclusion doctors had reached. The doctors' determination had ruled out any correctable causes for the arrhythmia. The ICD functioned by keeping track of my heart rate and rhythm. Thin wires connected the ICD to my heart so that it could detect and help prevent sudden death from occurring due to sudden cardiac arrest (which could potentially occur whenever there was sustained ventricular tachycardia or fibrillation) by delivering a shock to the heart.

The ICD operated by detecting an abnormal heart rate and rhythm. And whenever it detected one, the device would deliver to me an electric shock to restore a normal heartbeat when my heart is beating chaotically and too fast. It was very much needed because it gave me a shock on multiple occasions. The shocks happened suddenly, and the surprise of the shock would make me jump on numerous occasions. I compare a shock to the chest area to a sudden jolt; it is something similar to a very strong contact-shock impact. Other users have told me it felt like a kick in the chest for them, but not to me. I'm just glad it did the job it was supposed to do.

In spite of all the medications and extra measures, my heart continued to get weaker and weaker, and the ICD eventually begin to give more and more shocks. I eventually reached end stage heart failure.

And then another storm hit. My cardiologist gave me the shocking news that I would need to have a heart transplant, or my life expectancy would be greatly shortened. According to his calculation, I probably would not survive for more than two more years, if that, without a transplant. However, I was cautioned not to expect the heart transplant to occur quickly. In fact, no one knew exactly when it would take place (except, of course, God). But until I could receive a donor heart, a machine called a left ventricular assist device (LVAD), approved for the treatment of end stage heart failure, would be very helpful in assisting my heart to do its job.

The LVAD is a pump which was surgically implanted in my chest just below the heart; one end is attached to the left ventricle, the chamber of the heart that pumps blood that comes out of the lungs and into the body. The other end is attached to the aorta, the body's main artery, which is about a foot long and just over an inch in diameter. The blood that flows from the ventricles goes to the pump, which fills up, and when the LVAD's sensors indicate it is full of blood, that blood is ejected out of the device into the aorta, which is divided into four sections (but I will only go into detail about two). They are **1.** the ascending aorta, where coronary arteries branch off to supply the heart with blood; **2.** the aortic arch, which curves over the heart, giving rise to branches that bring blood to the head, neck, and arms. The other two are the descending thoracic aorta and the abdominal aorta. By doing the majority of the work, the LVAD allows the heart to have a chance to rest somewhat. The LVAD helped by relieving some of these symptoms such as being constantly tired or short of breath. It also improved other organ functioning, relieving some of my symptoms, and improved my exercise performance, which would enable me to participate in cardiac rehabilitation.

The LVAD was going to act as a bridge to heart transplantation until a compatible heart could become available, and this was something no one knew (except, of course, God).

God is able and wise to do what is best. (Proverbs 3:5)

The way the transplantation process was to work was that I first would have to be evaluated before being placed on a national waiting list, which is comprised of many other heart failure individuals and others waiting for various organs. I was to be ranked on the heart organ waiting list according to several different factors. For example there was a #1A list, a #1B list, and then a #2 list. I was first placed on a #2 list; then I progressed to a 1B list and finally moved to the 1A (top) list, which is among those on the first selection list. I would have to undergo several tests and be evaluated and approved by a slew of specialty doctors before being added initially to the #2 list and then advancing up to the #1B and then #1 lists.

The Atlanta doctor's prediction was that without a new heart or the temporary insertion of an LVAD, my life expectancy would be greatly shortened. As stated earlier, he predicted that without either I would probably have two years, if that, to live. Let me be transparent: that was a major head trip!!! It really shook my faith! The doctor's suggestion was for me to return to Chicago, where most of my family resided and where there was a great cardiologist, a friend of his, who practiced at a hospital not far from where I could live with one of my two sisters.

Behold. I am with you wherever you go, and will bring you back to this land. For I will not leave you until I have done what I promised you. (Genesis 28:15)

For we walk by faith, not by sight. (2 Corinthians 5:7)

Chapter 6

Should I Move Again, or Should I Stay?

The actual LVAD and its connections would have to be implanted during open-heart surgery. The hospital where the recommended new cardiologist was on staff was considered one of the renowned facilities for performing organ transplants and was considered among the premier hospitals for heart transplantation in the country.

Remember to trust in the Lord with all your heart and do not lean on your own understanding. (Proverbs 3:5)

I really did not want to leave Atlanta to return to Chicago, my hometown. I had relocated to Atlanta after leaving Miami, which is where I was first based as a Flight Attendant with Delta. I had made a new life in Atlanta. In addition, I was led to join a mega Baptist church where I got a "new birth", so to speak, gained a spiritual father and mother, and served at one time or another in various church ministries. I had even gone back to school and received a Bachelor of Theology degree in preparation for increased ministry work. In addition to the numerous friends I made in Atlanta, I also had three very close sister/ friends.

The thought of having to move back to Chicago made me feel somewhat like an Abraham in reverse, having to leave my new home to go back and live among relatives and a place I had originally left (Genesis 12:1).

There are times when God wants us to move.
We can all have a certain amount of baggage that we carry
from our past. Some of us have lighter loads than others.

Are you holding on to stuff that's blocking the move God
wants you to make?

I came to the understanding that it was necessary for me to forget, for the time being, what I was leaving behind or trying to hold onto. How could I press forward and higher unless I first learned how to let go of what was now the past? I had to press on towards the goal for the prize that would lead to the upward call of God in Jesus Christ. I was to move in order to prepare for a new calling and a new heart. If I had been disobedient, I could have delayed the greater destiny and blessing for a better life. I say, don't let your small thinking block your blessings. Trust the Lord and lean not to your own understanding (Proverbs 3:5).

Commit your way to the Lord, and Trust in Him. The Lord will keep you wherever you go. (Genesis 28:15, Proverbs 3: 5-6)

Deep down I knew I was going to have to go back to Chicago. I had to have the faith in God's plan and prayed that He would allow me to return to Atlanta as quickly as possible.

"I could feel The Lord saying to me, you have stayed long enough at this mountain." (Dt. 1:6)

I also realized it wouldn't be fair to expect friends to assist me with the level of care that I would require following my surgeries. Besides, the sister I was going to live with had recently retired from her job and had just finished working on her long awaited PhD in higher education, so she would be available to help me quite a bit. My younger sister, although still working, also planned to be available as much as possible to help. So it was back to Chicago for me. And with the assistance of an unbelievable, untiring circle of friends (especially Mrs. B.F. and her husband Mr. A.F. (with whom I was staying with at the time), and the help of Mr. W. M. and his wife C. M. (all of whom I shall be forever grateful to), I packed up only my necessities, and I flew back to Chicago. My nephew and a cousin volunteered to drive my SUV to Chicago for me.

In 2013, shortly after arriving in Chicago, I was scheduled to have the LVAD surgery performed. The actual LVAD and its internal connections were to be implanted during open-heart surgery, which was performed in October of 2013. A computer controller, a power pack which included a reserve power pack (or batteries), would remain outside my body.

The surgery was successful but came with some additional respiratory problems. As a result of these problems I had to be intubated for a short time. This necessitated me having a tracheostomy (a surgically created opening in the front of my neck where a tube was inserted into my trachea (windpipe), to which a ventilator was connected pumping oxygen rich air into my lungs to improve my breathing. While in place, I could not talk or eat and could not drink water or beverages (a real downer!). My trachea had to be suctioned via the actual tracheostomy tube, and the inner collar device of the trach tube had to be cleaned regularly by the nurses. Eventually, the tracheostomy tube and ventilator were removed; however, the opening in my neck remained until it closed on its own. I was a little worried that there would be a very noticeable external scar at the site as well as internal scar tissue which would obstruct the airway and require additional surgeries to clear out any blockage in the area. But, thanks to God, that did not happen and has not occurred to this day.

I learned not to worry about things I have no control over. It will only lead to anxiety. Life is much more important than the small things. (Matthew 6:25-34)

The LVAD surgery also necessitated an extended stay in the hospital for aftercare. During this time I underwent training relating to the

LVAD's operation, its care, familiarization with the LVAD's external parts, and participation in cardiac rehabilitation and physical therapy, as I also had additional body weakness resulting from the surgery.

The hospital assigned me a VAD Coordinator who was responsible for managing the care of the device as well as the exit site of the VAD connections, and for Coumadin management. The computer monitoring necessitated bi-monthly visits to the coordinator to evaluate how well the pump was operating as well as the coordinator overseeing regular INR testing—aka prothrobin time (PT) a blood test that measures how long it takes for the blood to clot. This was required because I was started on Coumadin, (a blood thinning drug). Also, while I was still in the hospital, my sister had to have training on how to perform special dressing changes for the driveline site of the LVAD (the line connection that led from the internal operating site of the pump), which protruded out of my lower abdomen on my left side. Care of this open site was a sterile procedure; it had to be done using a special sterile kit, gloves, and a face mask (worn by us both), and the site covered with a sterile dry dressing. Also, when discharged, I would be responsible for weighing myself daily, taking my vital signs, and taking and recording special VAD readings, recording all the results in a special binder.

I would require a lot of assistance not only following this surgery but also after the transplant, whenever it was performed.

This Heartware device (the LVAD) also necessitated that I wear the computer controller, along with the batteries, in a special bag that had a shoulder strap that held all this close to my body. It was important for me to be able to change over to another battery when one of the two ran out. I always had at least two extra batteries with me for unexpected emergencies or maybe even more batteries depending on how long I planned to be away from home. The batteries had to be recharged at night, and a backup generator had to be readily available in case of a power failure. In addition, I had to notify the fire department within my sister's community that I had the device in case I encountered a problem with it, and needed emergency transport to the hospital. All this meant I was in charge of guarding my own heart! All of these precautions were **very** important.

The Bible tells us to guard our heart with all diligence, because the heart determines the course of our life. (Proverbs 4:23)

For me, this was going to mean that I was guarding my heart both physically as well as spiritually.

For nothing is impossible with God. (Luke 1:37)

What good is it if you say you have faith, but do not have works? (James 2:14)

Chapter 7

A Greater Faith

Throughout this entire process I was, for a short time, questioning God. But all the enemy wanted to do was to steal, kill, sabotage, or destroy my belief in Christ (John 10:10).

I was being spiritually attacked by a lingering negativity that attempted to bring with it thoughts of being a failure and thoughts of never overcoming my challenging health problems and advancing to live an abundant life. This was a spiritual attack from the enemy. But his plan failed!

Listen for and faithfully obey the voice of the Lord your God, it is a blessing to you! (Deuteronomy 28:1)

Beware!!!The enemy will try to plant deceptive and negative thoughts in your mind.

This is an attempt to instill fear as well as attack your faith in God and any belief that He still has good plans for your life, in spite of everything you may be going through. I had to become more deeply engrossed in the Word, prayer, and fasting. With that came a renewing of the mind.

Stop trying to fight alone when going through a challenging time, know that He is God supreme over the whole world. God will rescue you. Keep faith, pray, read the Word, and fast to renew your mind. He is our defender and protector in whom we must trust. (Psalms 91:1-2).

If you are to successfully rise above any false and deceptive thoughts and feelings, I encourage you to seek to know the truth of God; once you know the truth, that truth will set you free by breaking any strongholds (John 8:32). There is a hope, a grace, and a revelation in Jesus Christ and the Word (Ephesians 4:23, 1 Peter 1:13).

Refocus, and keep in mind that Jesus conquered things in and of the world so that we could overcome them. (John 16:33)

Beware of the tricks of the enemy!!

Embrace your power and have peace. You already have victory over all the powers of the world through Jesus Christ. Remember, as I had to, that in spite of all you may be going through, keep in mind the importance of fighting negativity with the truth of the Word and continue in faith.

It's important to learn how to use the Word to fight

negativity and call the devil the liar he is.

Through Christ we are to have peace of mind. Don't forget that God has always thought of us as valuable and a product of His will and design. In Jesus we have the power to break every chain, stronghold, temptation, or whatever you choose to call it (2 Corinthians 10:3-5). We are to have and will have an abundant life because that is one of reasons why Jesus came. By the stripes of Jesus, our health, personal situations, and peace of mind can be restored.

You will be triumphant in any situation you may be battling.

By Jesus' sufferings He purchased for us the Spirit and grace of God (Isaiah 53:5).

Do you feel pain and frustration as I did as you wait for something new, positive, and different to happen in your life?

Do you feel as if all your hopes and dreams you envisioned for yourself are not going to materialize?

I know I did. Now contemplate this quote by Eleanor Roosevelt:

"The future belongs to those who believe in the beauty of their dreams." I add, and have faith in the beauty of Christ!

Rest assured, if you pray and ask God for understanding and patience to run your race, he will give you revelation after revelation that brings you peace concerning your future. He did it for me and He will do it for you. It will become clear in time as it did for me that what you consider to be a valley experience was in fact a time of testing, growth, and preparation for your mountaintop experiences.

I've discovered that adversities are temporary pit stops that come to make us stronger and wiser for the journey that lies ahead.

Think about Joseph, who spent a number of years in prison (a pit) before he was taken to the palace and given a position second to Pharaoh (Genesis 41:39-40). Remember, God gave Joseph grace and favor while he was in prison.

God holds restoration, and fulfillment of dreams. Don't lose yourself in despair; think about a bigger picture. The saying goes, "Change your thoughts, and you can change your life." It is possible to change bad thoughts. What are some possible ways God could be using your situation for good, just as He did for Joseph?

Our restoration may not be the way we expect it to be sometimes. Just as Joseph remained positive, I encourage you to remain positive and pregnant with God-inspired, limitless possibilities for your dreams as you go through challenging situations.

God is doing a new thing in your life, making a way in your perceived down time, and his purpose will take you from your pit to the palace as He did for Joseph.

Think about it, Joseph's challenges began after he had a dream! There are things we can't see which are wrapped up in our pit experiences because therein lies God's plan and purpose.

There's a blessing in your storm.

I discovered this and I urge you to believe that beneath your challenging situations, something new and good is springing forth. God is doing a new thing in your life as He is doing in mine, and what is perceived as a dry dark period is where a new flourishing oasis is going to spring forth (Isaiah 43:18-19).

Let God blow your mind!!

So forget the past, and don't dwell on it. Don't look in the rearview mirror of life or you will get a backward view.

Keep your eyes on the road ahead because that's the direction where you are headed and there's a better road ahead!

God gives us what we need. He has given us power within ourselves, so don't have a "woe is me" mentality.

Raise up and send the praise up!! Confuse the enemy.

"The past is history. The future, a mystery. The here and now is a gift. That is why it's called the present." ~Unknown

Chapter 8

The Gift of Life: The Present

I made it through. The storm has passed over and I'm still alive! The thief (of souls) thought to come only to steal, seize, or invade God's property through deception, false doctrine, or oppression: "But Jesus came that we, His sheep, may have life and have everything we need so that we can have life more abundantly" (John 10:10).

God's divine power has granted to me all things that pertain to life. (2 Peter 1:3)

Here I am, me, Janice Bentley, with a "new heart". I mean it in the physical sense. I had awaited my heart transplant approximately 1 year and 8 months (after the placement of the LVAD) until June 13, 2015, two days before my birthday; God's set time. I am now the recipient of a wonderful legacy passed to me through a person who registered to be an organ donor and whose family honored those wishes. Their intention was to bless others with the gift of a better life through their organ donation.

In August of 2016 I had the awesome opportunity to meet the donor's family. Initially, after receiving my transplant in 2015, I had asked the organization involved with organizing the availability of the organ to forward my thank you card to the family. In the card I also expressed my desire to meet them to personally thank them face to face for their loved one's selflessness to others. It was very important to me that they knew how truly grateful I am to have the heart of their loved one. I do not take my new heart lightly; I honor this heart and will do all I can to keep it healthy.

The donor's family[4] embraced me as soon as we met and I believe we all felt as kindred spirits. They are remarkable people, and as we talked during lunch I learned about the tragic circumstances surrounding the brain death of their loved one and about their life. The donor was a distinguished scholar beginning early in life and tragically lost life not long after graduating from one of the top five prestigious universities in the United States where they attended on a full scholarship.

God took tragedy and turned it into a continued triumph. And I plan to keep connected with them. Since our meeting, I have replayed one of the moments that was so powerful on that day. It was when they asked to feel the pulse of the heart and remarked that it had a strong beat. My new heart and I are getting along nicely with no signs of rejection. God knew exactly what He was doing and gave me a very good heart on multiple levels. I also now tease family and friends, telling

---

4. To protect the privacy of the donor's family, details here are intentionally vague.

them "I got a smart heart", and we just laugh.

I believe that the heart I received was a preordained act of grace by God. His preordained plan has always been to prosper me, not do me harm, but to give me hope and a future (Jeremiah 29:11).

There is a grace, hope, and revelation in Jesus Christ and the Word. (Ephesians 4:23, 1 Peter 1:13)

I know that God's preordained plan was that I prosper, not be harmed, but, that I inspire humanity by becoming an advocate for organ and tissue donations, as well as a messenger of hope for others (Jeremiah 29:11).

Through God's promises I have received and see the expectations of my faith in him, and He has done exceedingly and abundantly above that which is good and is fulfilling a purpose and plan He has for me. And by the way my new heart and I are getting along just fine!

God works all things together for the good of those who love Him, and are called, according to His purpose for them. (Romans 8:28)

We are all earthen vessels in the Potter's hands, we are on the Potter's wheel, and the Potter has power over the clay. The Potter can either allow any defects to remain or reshape the vessel to conform to His design (Jeremiah 18:3-6).

God reshapes broken vessels and turns them into valuable vessels that yield to His purpose. (Romans 9:20-24)

I was a broken vessel, and the Potter has reshaped me as seemed best to Him. Oh, there are more tests for me to endure. God's not finished yet. I'm still a work in progress being shaped by the Master for the purpose He has for my life. There is probably more reshaping for me to endure, and I will stay on the wheel until God is finished. As will you (Jeremiah 18:4).

As God's created vessel who are we to question God when He puts us (His vessels) back on His Potter's wheel and reshapes us? (Romans 9:20)

Will you trust God's reshaping of a broken vessel, making it more refined to suit His purpose? (Jeremiah 18:4)

God will fulfill the vision He has for you and me. We must trust Him to lead us to the right destination at the right time.

We can and will survive storms and lightning blasts. But before we let go and trust God, we can sometimes let the attacks of worry, fear, stress, and tension diminish our trust in God.

Beware of Spiritual Attacks. (Ephesians 6:10-18)

It's interesting to note that out of all of the words in the Bible, the word worry is not found.

Worry is not a word in God's vocabulary because worry is a silent killer!!

The thing is, when you worry, you're actually meditating. But you're meditating on the issues that disempower you. What you need to do is to meditate on God's word, for it empowers you.

Worry attacks you and disguises itself as "practical thinking." And one successful worry repellant I know is scripture meditation. That's because it's impossible to worry and meditate on God's Word and goodness at the same time. So take the time now and start memorizing and speaking God's promises.

Jesus is God's gift offering. He laid down His life for us, sacrificing himself, by taking our place so that we could be set free from the works of the enemy. This is the greatest blessing we can ever receive from God, and who doesn't like precious gifts?! Jesus is like a flawless diamond of unmeasurable wealth and one we cherish and hold onto for life. And we let no one take it away from us. Its brilliance illuminates us, giving us spiritual life while on the earth and eternally in the heavenly life hereafter. His grace brings us joy and happiness.

Stay with God that you will have life to its fullest. Resist the doctrine and tricks of the deceiver. (Ephesians 6:10-12)

The storms I have endured thus far have developed in me greater perseverance, strength, increased patience, and a greater awareness and understanding of who I am in Christ. I am and we are all more than a conqueror (overwhelmingly victorious) through Christ who loves us. I am confident that in spite of any storms we may encounter nothing can separate us from the love of God that is in Christ Jesus (Romans 8:37, 39).

Know that you will always be triumphant due to the power and the love God has for you! (Romans 8:37)

It's a fact: we can allow the storms of life to build us up, or, if we allow the enemy to cause us to worry, tear us down. Notice, I said *allow*. God gives us the power and courage to overcome adversity. Have the mindset that you are a conqueror in Christ Jesus (Romans 8:37). Jesus overcame the storms first, and the ultimate victory has already been won for us (John 16:33).

So, run your race. (1 Corinthians9: 24-27)

Wait on the Lord, He will renew your strength. (Isaiah40:31)

God's plan will come to pass in His appointed time. There is a specific time for everything (Ecclesiastes 3:1). Your time could be an instant victory or a very slow victory coming over time, as it did for me.

It's a fact God is never too early or too late.

If victory seems slow in coming, wait patiently, for it shall surely take place. For the revelation awaits an appointed time, and though it may linger, wait for it; it will certainly come and not be late (Habakkuk 2:3).

You can't change what has happened, but you can change how you allow it to affect you! You are being shaped by the Master for the purpose He has for you.

God's words are life to those who find them, and healing to all their flesh. (Proverbs 4:20-22)

Don't abort your spiritual baby. Stay the course, Push through your spiritual labor pains and deliver your inner Samson. God **IS** doing a new thing in your life. Do you not perceive it? (Isaiah 43:19). God is making a way in your perceived down time, and his purpose will take you from your pit to the palace as He did for Joseph (Gen.41:39-40).

There are things we can't see, things which are wrapped up in our pits, and therein lies His plan and purpose. There's a blessing in the storm. I discovered and I urge you to believe that beneath your challenging situations, whatever they are, there is something new. And what is perceived as a wasteland is new territory. Keep your eyes on the road ahead because that's the direction where you are headed!

We can all go through a process that can come to pass quickly or over the years, as it did for me. God is faithful; He will not give you more than you can bear! (1 Corinthians 10: 13)

In the world we will have trials and tribulations, but we must remain courageous. Remember, Jesus conquered the world so that we could overcome the world (John 16:33). We are to have peace and victory over all the powers of the world. We are not to let ourselves be overcome by the storms life presents.

All will go well if we keep the faith and, more importantly, learn how to use the Word to fight the storms we encounter in the world.

Through Christ we can have peace of mind. Remember, the deceiver wants to try to mess with our heads and trick us into forgetting that God has always thought of us as valuable and a product of His will and design.

In Jesus we have the power to break every chain, stronghold, temptation, storm of life, or whatever you choose to call it. We are to have an abundant life because that is one of the reasons why Jesus came. By the stripes of Jesus, we are healed in our body, mind, and spirit, and any situation we find ourselves in.

In Christ there is restoration. By Jesus' sufferings he purchased for us the Spirit and grace of God. (Isaiah 53:5)

God's grace that saves us is His free, underserved goodness and favor through faith in Christ Jesus. We are to sit in heavenly places raised above this world (Ephesians 2:6).

With deep studying, searching in the Word, through prayer, and listening to and meditating on God's Word, your truth

will surface.

Through revelation I know that no matter what the situation appears to be, trials serve as a time of preparation. Through trials we build up endurance for the greater purpose God has ordained for our life. Faith in God has encouraged me to run on until my destiny is fulfilled.

God is awesome! His Word is our sword, and faith in that Word is our shield.

The sun will shine in your life again. As I've stated before, you can't change what has happened, but you can change how you allow it to affect you! It's a fact we can allow the storms of our life to build us up or tear us down.

A person tested by adversity will grow and endure.

Your individual character and your life can be compared to the strength of a tree. After an intense storm, only the sturdiest trees are left standing. The harsher the wind, the stronger a tree must be in order to withstand it. Strong storms can destroy weaker vegetation. People who survive strong storms come to appreciate how their outlook has changed. They have a renewed appreciation for each and every day. They no longer get caught up with, or bothered by, things that don't really matter. It's important to maintain your focus on the big picture, which includes the direction and quality of your life, along with making progress towards your goals. Your level of satisfaction will increase while your stress decreases.

The deeper your roots are, the greater the challenges you can withstand. And each storm you successfully endure, it makes it easier to endure the next one.

Challenge and adversity are the winds that make you stronger. Trees that survive the most adverse weather conditions have developed deep roots and stout trunks. As you seek the Lord and overcome problems and difficulties, you develop in ways not otherwise possible.

Although you have within you everything needed to handle whatever may come your way, it takes a storm to bring your strengths to the surface.

If you worry, the storms of life will tear you down. God gives us the power and courage to overcome adversity.

You must have the mindset that you are a conqueror in Christ Jesus. (Romans 8:37)

We are always victorious because of the One who is our vindicator.

As a remedy against perplexing times, prayer is always the best defense. In this way, we show that we are acknowledging God's mercy and recognize our dependence on Him.

The Lord will deliver His people. As his flock, we are honored as jewels of his crown. Adversity can correct, spark change, spur on growth, and help us become better Christians. In the moment of it, adversity hurts, but later it yields peaceful fruit to those who have been trained by it (Hebrews 12:9-11). It's difficult to envision spiritual growth in the midst of pain. We can see our growth in retrospect, but while experiencing pain we will seek to try to return to our comfortable pain-free and growth-free state.

Remember to fear the Lord, don't get caught up in evil; and don't be wise in your own understanding, let God be healing to your flesh and refreshment to your bones. (Proverbs 3:5-8)

Bless the Lord, O my soul and forget not all His benefits, make known His deeds, let the whole world know what He has done. (Psalms 103:2, 1 Chronicles 16:8-9)

Glory belongs to God, whose power is at work in us. By this power He can do infinitely more than we can ask or imagine. (Ephesians 3:20)

Chapter 9
The Future

Because Christ is in us, there is a power that is active within us. We have a responsibility to help others understand and know Christ so that they may be led to accept, reverence, and appreciate Him. Let's not dwell on the past. Instead, let us grow in the knowledge of Christ by concentrating on our relationship with Him now.

I strive not to dwell on the past, but instead look forward to a fuller, newer, and more meaningful life because of my hope in Christ. I got it!! I have a responsibility and an everlasting covenant in Christ. See, I know, without a shadow of a doubt, Christ is all over and in me. This understanding is much more firmly embedded in my belief system. And I am moving on to a life of increased faith and obedience. I press on toward the goal to win the prize God intends for me to receive (Philippians 3:12-13).

The heart of man plans his way, but the Lord establishes his steps! (Proverbs 16:9)

I don't know what tomorrow will bring or what my life is to be. But I do know life is too short not to do what I know I should do. And that's to live life according to God's plan. I believe it's good to have goals and plans, but our goals and plans can disappoint us if we leave God out of them. God holds our future in His hands. I will live my life doing whatever He has planned for me.

They who wait for the Lord shall renew their strength; they shall mount up with wings like eagles, they shall run and not get weary, they shall walk and not get faint. (Isaiah 40:31)

I can't take my eyes off the goal. I want to have a more intimate relationship with Christ. I will always seek to let go of anything that tries to distract me from being a more effective useful vessel for Christ. It is my hope to be able to bring others into the marvelous revelation of Jesus Christ the hope of glory. (Colossians 1:27).

As I ponder the following question I invite you to do the same: *What's holding you back?*

In order to move forward, I will continue to study to get a greater understanding of the life and teachings of Christ (Matthew 11:29). I am studying, praying, and allowing the Holy Spirit to teach and refresh my understanding of Jesus' teachings and words. I trust the Holy Spirit to plant the truth in my mind, convince me of God's will, and remind me when I'm straying from it. God is perfecting good works in me, and the highest honor for me is to be in the service of the Lord.

There will be more for me to successfully endure because God is not finished yet. And I believe that we all are works in progress, being shaped by the Master for the purpose He has for our lives. Just as weather-related storms can sometimes be devastating, they can bring new development and rebuilding. For me it built greater perseverance, increased patience, obedience to God, and a greater awareness of whom I am in Christ. Through faith and situational reinforcement, a solid foundation based on trust and God's perfect timing has been established (Ecclesiastes 3:1).

Think about your situation. Get a greater picture and purpose for your life!

I believe, what's happening to you as it was for me is a time of preparation and spiritual growth that will build in you a greater faith in God's promises. Have faith and hold on for the greater purpose God has ordained for your life.

Sin, fear, uncertainty, doubt, and other forces are attempting to war within us.

God's peace resides there in our hearts and lives to restrain hostile forces and offers comfort in place of conflict. To me, it's more about seeking a stronger relationship with God where there is Godly understanding and agreement in all things, or of one mind. I choose not to allow myself to be troubled by or afraid of what my future holds. I'm learning more and more how to dwell in the peace that Christ gives.

Our faith, our conversion, and our eternal salvation are not a result of any one thing that we have done but by the free gift of God.

Through God's preparation and through his Holy Spirit, a change is produced in our lives, and we have a responsibility to glorify Him and persevere in holiness.

If we give God what we have, no matter how little and ineffective we may think it is, God will use it.

It is our availability God wants. It makes us alive to God. We have a new moral life. Let us glorify Him in our deeds and our actions. We have been bought with a price (Romans 8:18).

Know that in all things God works for the good of those who love Him, and who have been called according to His purpose. (Romans 8:28)

I urge you to see all the possibilities, not the problems. It is by grace we have been saved, and it is not of our own doing; it is the gift of God (Ephesians 2:6-8).

Remember, don't abort your spiritual baby, but push through your labor pains, and deliver your inner Samson.

There's a blessing in the storm. I discovered and I urge you to believe that beneath your challenging situations, whatever they are, something new and positive is developing.

What is perceived as a wasteland is new territory and new opportunity for growth.

Sooner or later we all will experience a potential destructive storm in our front yard. For this reason, our choice as the foundation for a survival plan must be Christ, who can help us weather all storms. With Him, we will withstand the full force of even the strongest storms. And although we may be subjected to challenging circumstances we continue to stand strong, flourish, and persevere.

Be a survivor! As the Timex watch slogan used to say "It takes a licking and keeps on ticking".

Be so durable and flexible that you can handle the very worst with relatively minor, if any damage, and bend without breaking.

I learned and let me encourage you to:

Hope in the Lord and He will renew your strength, you will soar on wings like eagles, you will run on and not get weary. (Isaiah 40:31)

You will go on. God's grace is available to you; He helps those who are in humble dependence on him. Rest assured, if you pray and ask God for understanding and patience to run your race, as I said before,

He will give you revelation after revelation that brings peace concerning your situation. He did it for me, and He will do it for you.

Remember that though we are weak, we are actually strong. God's grace is all we need because His power is perfected when we are weak.

Paul tells us in 2 Corinthians 12:9 that he would joyfully boast in his own sufferings that the power of God may rest upon him.

Know that whatever you may be going through, or will go through, God's strength will get you through it.
(2 Corinthians 12:9)

Allow God's providence to be a great source of comfort in trying times. The Lord will deliver His people. I repeat, as his flock, we are honored as jewels of his crown. The adversity that we encounter can correct us, spark change in us, spur on growth, and help us become better people enduring what is sometimes uncomfortable.

It's difficult to chart spiritual growth in the midst of pain. But we can see growth in retrospect.

Being open to God's plan for your life means that everything will become clear in time.

Christ's peace gives confident assurance that resting in Him, in whatever circumstances we find ourselves, we will always be ***Victorious*!!**

May God Bless You!

In the will of Christ,

J.B. (Newheart 6.13.2015)

I pray that you are encouraged. Please write me at Janice@JaniceBentley.com. I'm very interested in knowing how this book has impacted you.

An Invitation

If you do not know Christ and have not accepted Him as your Lord and Savior I invite you to pray the following prayer of Salvation: For whoever calls on the name of the Lord shall be saved! (Ro. 10:13)

Dear Lord Jesus,
I know I am a sinner, and I ask for your forgiveness.
I believe you died for my sins and rose from the dead.
I trust and follow you as my Lord and Savior. Guide
my life and help me to do your will.
In Jesus name,
Amen

You are invited to find and join a Bible-based Church that will help you learn, mature, and guide you in your Christian walk. I also invite you to join the International prayer call and prayer warriors led by my pastor and spiritual father Bishop Eddie L. Long of New Birth Missionary Baptist Church along with Bishop Kenneth Pearman of the Reaching out for Jesus Christian Center, Mon.-Fri at 6:30 am Eastern time, by dialing 641-715-3572 or 641-715-3573. You will have a blessed experience! Prayer requests can be submitted by sending an email with your requests to MorningPrayer @Newbirth.org.

APPENDIX

Heart

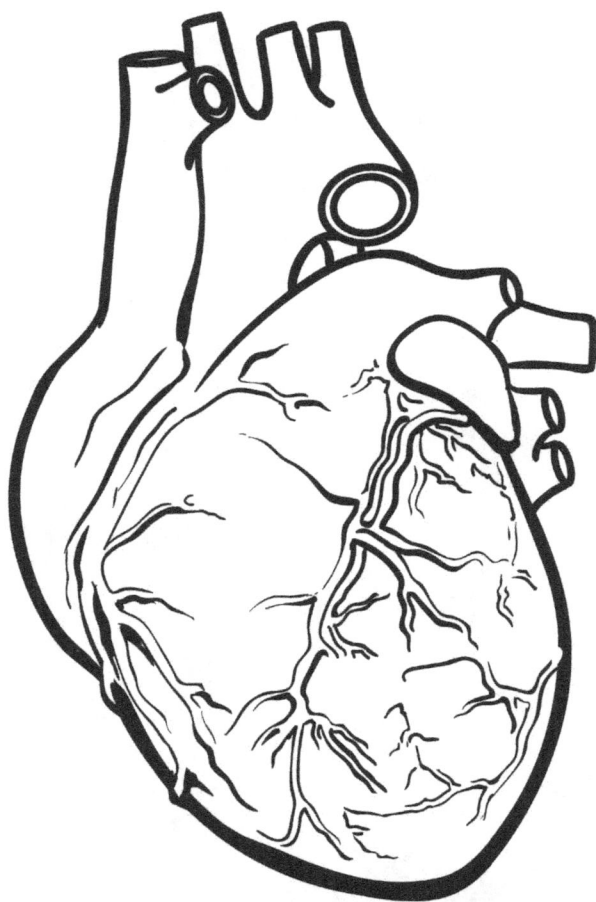

According to history provided to the public by UNOS (United Network for Organ Sharing), the first successful adult human-to-human heart transplant was done by Dr. Norman Shumway on January 6, 1968, at the Stanford University Hospital in Palo Alto, California. Dr. Shumway is widely regarded as the father of heart transplantation. Presently, it has been estimated that worldwide, about 3,500 heart transplants are performed annually. The vast majority of these are performed in the United States (**approximately 2,000-2,300**) annually.[56]

Dr. Shumway's patient was a 54-year-old man who received the heart of a 43-year-old man. Unfortunately, the recipient died fifteens days later of multiple systemic complications[7].

As stated in "A Brief History of Heart Transplantation" found on the Columbia University Department of Surgery website, in the 20 years following the 1968 transplant surgery, "important advances in tissue typing and immunosuppressant drugs allowed more transplant operations to take place and increased patients' survival rates. The most notable development in this area area was microbiologist Jean Borel's discovery of cyclosporine, an immunosuppressant drug derived from soil fungus in the mid 1970's." This development of better anti-rejection drugs made transplantation more viable and dramatically expanded

5. "Heart Transplantation." Wikipedia, 2016. www.wikiwand.com/en/Heart_transplantation. Accessed 6 September 2016.
6. "First successful heart transplant in the United States." The 1968 Exhibit: Timeline, January, 2016. the1968exhibit.org/1968-timeline/January. Accessed 6 September 2016.
7. Ibid.

a transplant patient's life expectancy[8].

According to the latest national statistics on survival rates following heart transplantation, success rates have revealed[9]

- **90% survival rate at 1 year,**
- **75% survival rate at 5 years,**
- **50% survival rate at 12 years.**

However, long-term success exceeding **25** years of survival is possible. Today's greatest challenge to successful heart transplant surgery continues to be finding donors, which is **<u>extremely</u>** difficult.

- Currently, the demand for organ, eye, and tissue donation vastly exceeds the number of donors!
- Sadly, on average, 22 people die each day while waiting for a life-saving transplant due to the severe shortage of organ donations! [10]
- As of 6/30/16, there are slightly over 120,000 people in the United States waiting for a lifesaving transplant, and they depend on gifts

8. "A Brief History of Heart Transplantation". Columbia University Department of Surgery: Cardiac Transplant Program, 2016. http://columbiasurgery.org/heart-transplant/brief-history-heart-transplantation. Accessed 6 September 2016.

9. "Heart Transplant Outcomes." Barnes Jewish Hospital: Heart Failure and Heart Transplant Program, 2016. http://www.barnesjewish.org/Medical-Services/Transplant/Heart-Transplant/Heart-Transplant-Outcomes. Accessed 6 September 2016.

10. "About Tissue and Organ Donation: Stats and Facts." Gift of Hope Organ & Tissue Donor Network, 2015. http://www.giftofhope.org/about_donation/trends_and_waiting_list.htm. Accessed 6 September 2016.

of selfless generosity from people just like you! [11]

- Every **10** minutes someone is added to the National Transplant Waiting List. [12]

- After death, an individual that has signed up to become an organ donor has the ability to save **8** lives. And that same donor, by donating tissues and eyes, can also save or improve the lives of up to **25** people. [13]

- Organ donations can include the following: heart, heart valves, kidneys, pancreas, lungs, liver, and the small intestine. [14] [15]

- Tissue donations include the following: cardiovascular and musculo-skeletal tissue, blood, bone marrow, skin, bones, tendons, ligaments, cartilage, veins, and the cornea. [16]

- After death, just about all people, with some exceptions (determined by donor specialists at the time of the donation), can be considered as potential organ and tissue donors.

11. "Local and National Waiting Lists: As of 6/30/16." Gift of Hope Organ & Tissue Donor Network, 2015. http://www.giftofhope.org/about_donation/trends_and_waiting_list.htm. Accessed 6 September 2016.
12. "About Tissue and Organ Donation: Stats and Facts." Gift of Hope Organ & Tissue Donor Network, 2015. http://www.giftofhope.org/about_donation/trends_and_waiting_list.htm. Accessed 6 September 2016.
13. Ibid.
14. "FAQs about Donation: What organs and tissues can be donated?" Gift of Hope Organ & Tissue Donor Network, 2015. http://www.giftofhope.org/about_donation/faqs_about_donation.htm. Accessed 6 September 2016.
15. "Facts about organ donation." United Network for Organ Sharing, 2015. https://www.unos.org/donation/. Accessed 6 September 2016.
16. Ibid.

Consider leaving a legacy that will benefit humanity! Become an organ or tissue Donor! You have the power to save or enhance someone's life!!

Organ donation can be one of the greatest legacies you can leave to humanity. Signing up is fast and easy and can be done in the comfort of your home online, or you can sign up at the Department of Motor Vehicles in your state. There are also websites where you can go for more information about becoming a donor and sign up. I have listed only a few here:

- Organdonor.gov/donor-registry
- www.giftofhope.org
- www.donatelife.net
- www.unos.org

As stated, these are just a few websites where you can go to sign up to become an organ or tissue donor, but there are more. *"Both deceased and some types of living organ donation begins with a person who recognizes an opportunity to help others."* No matter your age, you can be an organ or tissue donor. Donors under 18 years of age must have a parent or adult guardian's signature for it to be legal. Your medical condition at the time of death will determine what organs and tissue can be donated as determined by a medical specialist. [17]

17. "Facts about organ donation." United Network for Organ Sharing, 2015. https://www.unos.org/donation/. Accessed 6 September 2016.

"Even if you have indicated your wishes on your driver's license or in a national or state registry be sure to share your decision with your family so they know and understand your wishes!" [18]

By registering to become a donor and donating, imagine what you can make possible for someone who desperately needs you!

It's all about giving back isn't it? And you'll be leaving a legacy that will benefit humanity...THE GIFT OF LIFE!

There's a quote by Randy Travis that says, "It's <u>not</u> what you take when <u>you</u> leave this world behind you. It's what <u>you</u> leave behind when <u>you</u> go!

I leave you with this thought. When you go to your final resting place *you* won't need your *organs,* but some of the people remaining will! *So please, won't you help? Sign up to become an organ donor!!*

Thank you and God bless!

Honored to be an advocate,

Sincerely,

Janice Bentley

---

18. "Facts about organ donation." United Network for Organ Sharing, 2015. https://www.unos.org/donation/. Accessed 6 September 2016.

Acknowledgements

First and foremost, Thanks be to God who inspired me to share my journey and lessons learned with others. I give him praise, honor, and all the glory! He is so awescme!!!

I am forever grateful to both my parents, James L. Bentley, Sr. and Willa Mae Bentley, who are responsible for my conception and nurturing. Mom you were great, you carried me, and delivered me. I know I must have loved you right from the start. And although you are gone to your eternal resting place with the Lord, I honor your memory. You will forever be a part of me.

And in remembrance and acknowledgement to Leola E. Haynes my maternal grandmother, who has gone on to be with the Lord but played a pivotal role in my personal development.

Thanks to all my family, especially my siblings: sister Marianne Stallworth, who took care of my early special health needs after my surgeries and continues to assist me now; sister Cheryl Bentley, who unselfishly continues to look after my Suv and give me special surprise treats.

I'm eternally grateful to my heart donor family, who God used to give me their gift of life.

Thanks to all the medical professionals, especially the Heart Transplant team, and other doctors and coordinators in Chicago who took fantastic care of me in and out of the hospital.

Thanks to those whose expertise helped me get this book edited, formatted, marketed, and published.

A special thank you to all my Atlanta friends, but especially Brenda and, Art who continue to have my back, and also Willie, Chanel, Felicia, Michael and Linda.

I'm grateful for Bishop Long, first Lady Long, and the New Birth Health Ministry and other church members, much love!

There are many, many others; you know who you are. God bless you for everything!